Work at Home Wisdom

WORK AT HOME WISDOM

David H. Bangs, Jr.
and Andi Axman

Upstart
Publishing Company®
Specializing in Small Business Publishing
a division of Dearborn Publishing Group, Inc.

Acquisitions Editor: Danielle Egan-Miller
Managing Editor: Jack Kiburz
Interior Design: Lucy Jenkins
Cover Design: Scott Rattray, Rattray Design
Typesetting: the dotted i

Published by Upstart Publishing Company®,
a division of Dearborn Publishing Group, Inc.

Printed in the United States of America

98 99 00 10 9 8 7 6 5 4 3 2 1

Library of Congress Cataloging-in-Publication Data

Bangs, David H.
Work at home wisdom : a collection of quips, tips, and inspirations to balance work, family, and home / David H. Bangs, Jr. and Andi Axman.
p cm.
ISBN 1-57410-100-5 (pbk.)
1. Home-based businesses—Quotations, maxims, etc. 2. Home labor—Quotations, maxims, etc. 3. Work and family—Quotations, maxims, etc. I. Axman, Andi. II. Title.
HD62.38.B36 1998
658′.041—dc21 98-28294
CIP

CONTENTS

ACKNOWLEDGMENTS

We'd like to give special thanks to the following:

- Our spouses, Lacey Bangs and Mark Goldstein, for making our homes wonderful places to live and work
- Our beloved dogs—Thud, a black Labrador retriever, and Ruby, a Chesapeake Bay retriever—for their wagging tails and constant companionship
- Danielle Egan-Miller, our acquisitions editor at Dearborn Financial Publishing, for encouraging us to write this book
- Our CPAs, Gerry Weidema and Stephen C. Robinson, for minding our businesses
- All of our clients and colleagues, for sharing their experiences with us, without which we could not have written this book

PREFACE

We were asked to write this little book by Danielle Egan-Miller, our editor at Dearborn Financial Publishing, as a companion to our book *Launching Your Home-Based Business.* We all agreed that a book touching on the emotional, personal side of working at home would provide a welcome balance to the more practical and businesslike approach of our other books. Hence *Work at Home Wisdom.*

We have both worked from our homes for years. Andi is a highly respected freelance writer and editor, working from her home in rural Epsom, New Hampshire. She had previously been an editor of financial newsletters and an entrepreneur with her own publishing venture. She's been there! She understands what it is to be a home worker with a sporadic income and erratic work flow.

And so does Andy. He started his own publishing company back in 1976 as a home-based business, involving his children in such exciting chores as collating newsletters and stuffing envelopes. Upstart rapidly outgrew his dining room into leased space. When he sold it in 1991, he went back to working at home as a writer, investor, and speaker. Right now, his office is in downtown Portsmouth, New Hampshire, though he still spends about half his working hours at home.

We've attempted to put our experiences at your disposal. Our "wisdom" is grouped loosely into chapters, so you can find an appropriate quote to brighten your day or an anecdote to illumine a problem. This is not a how-to book. Think of it as a personal tool kit for being a home-based worker.

We wish you as much luck and joy in your work as we have found. Working at home has its ups and downs, but we have found that the ups make the downs worthwhile.

Good luck, fellow home workers!

—Andi Axman and David H. "Andy" Bangs

CHAPTER 1

WELCOME HOME!

There's no place like home!

—Dorothy in L. Frank Baum's The Wizard of Oz

Whether you've said good-bye to your corporate cubicle forever or only for a day or two each week, it won't take long before you agree with Dorothy—even if you know nothing about cows, tornadoes, little dogs, or Kansas.

Today, nearly one-third of the workforce in America works at home either full-time or part-time, according to IDC/Link Resources, a private research firm in New York City. And that number is expected to grow steadily into the 21st century and beyond as we redefine the way we work.

The benefits of working from home are real: no time spent commuting, dressing as casually as you want, being on hand for family members and pets, having more time to focus on work with fewer distractions, being able to make phone calls from your deck or garden, doing your work when it fits in to your schedule, and, most important, making the kind of coffee you like to drink.

All of our dreams can come true—
if we have the courage
to pursue them.

—*Walt Disney*

Do you long to get out of the office for a few days every week so you can do the work you love to do—or absolutely have to do? Do you dream of giving up your day job and starting your own business? Or are you working harder than ever despite being retired—and loving every minute of it, except for the fact that you can no longer dine at your dining room table?

So where do you pursue your venture? You needn't look any further than home sweet home. All sorts of work-at-home ventures have been launched from a kitchen or dining room table. That's where both of us embarked on our writing careers.

If space is at a premium in your house or apartment, look for a spare corner to set up a work space. A hallway nook or even a closet minus its doors can easily accommodate a desk. Screens can divide a larger room into home and office space. Maybe you've got an extra bedroom or a section in the basement that's never used for anything except to collect clutter. Just make sure that basement and attic spaces have adequate ventilation, lighting, and temperature control. For inspiration in setting up your home office, see *Home Office Computing*'s monthly articles on office design.

Well begun is half done.

—*Aristotle*

Organization is the key to success in working at home. To keep everyone in your household sane and on speaking terms, aim to keep work confined to your office and everything else confined to your home. But for most of us who work at home, that can be easier said than done.

Set up an office with a door you can close behind you when you "go home." If that's not possible, use a room divider or a self-contained computer workstation with doors.

Make good use of every inch of your home office by getting the most space possible out of bookshelves, closets, and file cabinets. Be ruthless with paper by keeping only this year's paperwork in your office. In an easily accessible spot, store tax returns less than seven years old, insurance policies, legal documents, medical records, and warranties for office equipment. Throw away everything you no longer need.

One thing you'll want to make room for is houseplants, which, aside from looking nice, can improve the quality of air you breathe. According to *How to Grow Fresh Air* by B.C. Wolverton (Penguin Books, 1997), the bamboo palm, rubber plant, English ivy, and corn plant are particularly good at purifying the air and are easy to care for.

The buyer has need
of a hundred eyes,
the seller of but one.

—Italian proverb

Although it's fun to fantasize while shopping or reading *Office Beautiful,* most of us who are furnishing and equipping a home office have to work with a budget.

There are many routes to go for furniture: brand-spanking-new versus yard-sale specials, Office Max chic versus grandma's antiques, some of each, and everything in between. You may even want to invest in furniture made just for you, like the standing desk Andy ordered from Homeworks in Pittsfield, Maine (800-851-4777). But one luxury worth splurging on is your chair. Because the average office worker spends 75 percent of his or her time sitting, seating is the single most important aspect of creating a productive office.

How do you choose a good chair? First, never buy it through the mail. Visit a dealer showroom and sit in the chair for a few minutes to see if it fits you. Second, look for a lever that adjusts the height of the chair, an adjustable seat, a padded backrest and spinal support, padded armrests, and dual wheel casters.

As you set up your home office, try to create a space that will nurture both you and your work.

Remember that
time is money.

—Benjamin Franklin

One of the biggest joys of working at home is the short commute from home to work. Hours spent on the road traveling from home to office and back quickly add up. From November to March, those hours can double or triple for commuters here in New England and other environs in the Great White North. That's a lot of time lost sitting in traffic.

Because time is a home worker's most valuable asset, make the most of yours when you have to travel for work by listening to books on tape. (Those of you lucky enough to have access to mass transit can read the real thing.) Use a tape recorder to record memos to yourself and others.

Andi's become a devotee of the cell phone—her home office is off the beaten path and some days find her spending hours in her car. She has peace of mind knowing she's never more than a phone call away from anyone or anyplace—and has the phone bills to prove it.

A penny saved
is a penny got.

—George Washington

In general, it costs a lot less to work at home than it does to work anywhere else. For those of us nurturing a home-based business, home affords the luxury of stretching every dollar to its maximum. We have no rent to pay, we can get away without spending extra for a business phone line, and we don't have to dish out that much more for utilities. An astonishing 45 percent of the companies in the 1996 *Inc.* 500 list were started in their founder's residence, spending an average of 13 money-saving months at home.

And few among us needs a wardrobe budget comparable to that of our corporate comrades. Every day is "dress down" day, as far as we're concerned, except for those occasions when we have to make a fashion statement to impress a colleague or client. And even better than saving money on comfortable work clothes that don't have to be dry-cleaned is that the women among us don't have to shell out unlimited dollars for vast pantyhose reserves. Because we're less likely to wear them, they're less likely to rip; therefore, we need fewer of them. For Andi, that's *the* major benefit of working at home.

Let freedom ring.

—Samuel Francis Smith

Where else but home can you get in a few games of solitaire, play with your dog, or call friends without worrying that someone's looking over your shoulder? For many of us home workers, independence is at the core of our values.

One of the biggest advantages we have is that we can set our own work schedules. If 9-to-5 is your ideal work day, fine. But if your creative juices don't start flowing until 9 PM, that's fine, too, provided you get your work done in the time frame allotted. If you happen to do eight hours' work in six, give yourself a big pat on the back and "go home" early. Voice mail and answering machines make "face time" a nonissue for home workers.

Having control over your work schedule is actually good for you, according to British researchers who reported that lack of control over work life can cause heart disease. Here's to your health!

May you have warmth
in your igloo,
oil in your lamp,
and peace in your heart.

—*Eskimo proverb*

When it comes to creature comforts, there's just no place like home to work. Within sprinting distance is a fridge ready to lure you from work at a moment's notice. "Telecommuters can eat any time they want, just like wild animals," muses the growing-in-girth telecommuter Alice in a *Dilbert* comic strip.

You can listen to music if you want, and bring your dog to work—of utmost importance to both of us, neither of whom likes working any other way. Your work space can be painted whatever color you like and decorated in any style you find appealing. You can keep your office or studio as tidy as you want to—or not—and at a temperature that you find comfortable. After not having to wear nylons to work, Andi's second-most favorite aspect of working at home is that she's in control of the thermostat.

CHAPTER 2

THE JOY OF WORKING AT HOME

Perfect freedom is reserved
for the man who lives
by his own work
and in that work
does what he wants to do.

—R.G. Collingwood

If you yearn to work on your own either part-time or full-time, pay attention to your dreams. They tell you a lot about what you like (and don't like) to do.

Some of you may long to write, like we always had. Andy took the plunge from a banking career into publishing, starting a business at his dining room table and growing it so that it eventually moved to larger quarters and employed a dozen full-timers. Although Andi has been working solo for years, her office has graduated from the dining room table in her apartment to a room all its own in her house.

No matter what kind of work you dream of doing, take time to do wishful thinking/constructive daydreaming. Keep a journal and write down your thoughts for at least five minutes every day. To help you take inventory of your skills, likes, and dislikes, read *What Color Is Your Parachute?* by Richard Nelson Bolles (Ten Speed Press, 1998). To help you decide if self-employment is for you, see our quiz on pages 12 to 21 in *Launching Your Home-Based Business* (Upstart Publishing Company, 1998).

Life without industry is guilt.
Industry without art is brutality.

—William Morris

Life without industry (work, in this case) is also boring. Morris was an English artist and craftsman concerned with the deadening effects of 19th-century factory life. He pointed out that work and art should go together, that the workplace and the artifacts produced by that workplace should be influenced by art.

Apply this to your home office or workplace. There's no rule (except a lingering puritanism) that dictates a barren workscape. Andy hangs pictures of boats, calendars, photos he likes, interesting book covers, and other strange items on his walls. Andi is more artistic. She insists on flowers and interesting *objets d'art* to rest her eyes and mind upon.

And of course we both have our dogs working with us. Can Labrador and Chesapeake Bay retrievers be considered works of art? Why not?

Freud claimed that work and love are what makes life worthwhile, and that maturity is shown by a capacity to work and to love.

A woman must have money
and a room of her own
if she is to write fiction.

—Virginia Woolf

To do a good job working at home, you must have the space conducive to doing so. Although you don't necessarily need a whole room to yourself, you do need a way to ensure quiet and privacy when you need it. Room dividers and waiting until you have the house to yourself work well. So does having a separate building to house your studio or office, like our friend Joni Doherty, a graphic designer and painter whose 1,000-square-foot studio gives her room to pursue all her interests under one roof.

Setting up a home office also requires a financial investment. There are equipment, tools, office supplies, furniture, decorations, and everything else you'll need to make your office a comfortable and productive space. Business owners will have additional expenses, like business cards and letterhead and monthly overhead. Where will you get the money to support your home office? Whether it's generated by your business, a part-time job, the full-time employer who allows you to telecommute, a significant other or spouse, or an oil well in Texas, make sure you have enough cash so that you're spending time focusing on your work—not worrying about making ends meet.

Moderation,
the noblest gift of heaven.

—Euripides

One of the biggest advantages of working at home is that you can set your own hours. You can work the standard 9:00 AM to 5:00 PM if you wish, or from 6:00 PM to 2:00 AM if that's what suits you.

But who among us doesn't feel the temptation to work just a little bit longer, to get just a little more done? The Bureau of Labor Statistics reports that employed women are working 233 more hours a year than in 1976, while men are working 100 hours more. Under pressure to make more money, to get ahead, to get more done with fewer resources, and so on, we all have to be on the lookout for that slippery slope descending from hard work to workaholism and ultimately to burnout.

The red flag is already up for home-based business owners. Statistics say we work, on average, a 53-hour week instead of the typical American's 47-hour work week. Working hard may be fun and can do us lots of good on our career paths—but only if we maintain a balance between work, family, and home.

When there was an
important job to be done,
Everybody was asked to do it.
Anybody could have done it,
but Nobody did.
Somebody got angry about that
because it was Everybody's job.
Everybody thought Anybody could
do it, but Nobody realized that
Everybody wouldn't do it.
Consequently, it wound up that
Nobody told Anybody, so
Everybody blamed Somebody.

—*Anonymous*

Remember when you worked with a lot of other people? Much of management's time was spent creating and supporting systems to make sure that this kind of noncommunication didn't happen.

Just because you now work at home, it doesn't follow that this type of problem is behind you. More than one small family crisis comes about because Mother or Father says, "The lawn has to be raked," or "The table needs to be set." Everybody hears it; nobody acts on it. More direct forms of communication work better, and can prevent misunderstandings.

If you can't stand solitude,
maybe you bore others, too.

—*Bob Gordon*

No matter how you slice it, working at home is a quiet endeavor. It can be a boon for those of us who enjoy some solitude and crave uninterrupted time to concentrate on our work. However, it shouldn't be too quiet of a time.

If you're a telecommuter who feels isolated from your buddies at the office or a home-based business owner convinced that your ability to chitchat is eroding on a daily basis, we have two words of advice: Make connections. Stay in the loop with your coworkers and colleagues by picking up the phone, sending e-mail, or making a lunch date. And read Chapter 5 in this book ASAP.

A place for everything,
and everything in its place.

—Isabella Beeton

One way to make the most of your time in your home office is to keep it well organized. For many people who work and live in the same place, that's a lot easier said than done, especially when the work space is in the bedroom, on the dining room table, or in a corner of the family room.

Start by making a rule that work never leaves your office, unless, of course, it's going out the door for good. On the other hand, it's perfectly all right to allow your personal life to encroach on your home office—in fact, the more, the better. For example, it's a welcome relief for Andi to find the latest issue of *Saveur* and some dog toys in her office, but work-in-progress near her couch is *verboten* because of its harmful effect on watching movies.

Keep your work confined to the office. Shut the door behind you, either literally or figuratively, and take a break to relax or do something else you enjoy doing. You'll thank yourself later.

Have a place for everything
and keep the thing
somewhere else.
This is not advice,
it is merely custom.

—Mark Twain

Try as we do to maintain some order in our lives, the reality of the situation is that no matter how well organized we are, it's downright hard to keep work and home spaces completely separate. Things move around and disappear from their preordained places, then magically reappear somewhere where you'd least expect them. You don't need young children in order for entropy to reign supreme—just have several houseguests visit for a week and see what happens to your home, office included. Or go away for a few days, granting access to your office to your spouse or significant other. Chances are pretty good that something won't be where you expect to find it at the precise moment when you desperately need it.

There are times when Andi gets sick of the piles of paper throughout her house—mail, magazines, and newspapers on the kitchen counter, on the kitchen table, on the coffee table, on the stairs en route to her office, in her office, and so on. Every now and then, she'll devote a good part of a day to downsizing those piles, catching up on her reading and correspondence, and recycling or trashing as much paper as possible. Coincidentally, these days always fall a few days prior to her mother's visits.

Energy and persistence conquer all things.

—Benjamin Franklin,
Poor Richard's Almanac

No one who works at home would disagree that it takes work to be able to work at home. Besides setting up an office, you have to make sure it continues to run to your satisfaction. Then there are the unforeseen distractions, interruptions, and other problems that can be terrific drains of your time, your energy, and your cash.

Keep a list of helpers you can call on when problems do arise—a computer wizard, a public relations expert, a specialist in finance and accounting. If a problem-solving approach doesn't work or a strategy fails, don't give up. Rome wasn't built in a day, and neither were any professional ventures. Keep yourself hale and hearty, eat well and get your rest, and hang in there when times get tough. Those, too, as the old saying goes, will pass away.

CHAPTER 3

JUGGLING WORK, HOME, AND FAMILY

Ginger Rogers did everything
Fred Astaire did.
She just did it backwards
and in high heels.

—Ann Richards, in her keynote address to the 1988 Democratic National Convention

When we give workshops for women who are considering going into business for themselves or reentering the workforce after years spent raising a family, they often tell us that they have no marketable skills. Baloney! Pfui! Of course you have skills, we reply. Think of the jobs you have performed capably: scheduling; organizing and managing family activities; motivating and coaching; managing finances; setting budgets; delegating; being a board member and working on a committee for civic or charitable organizations; and multitasking. (How many things can you do at once? Lots!)

This list can be expanded, but you get the point. The skills and judgment required to manage a household are very similar to those required to manage a business or to work as an independent employee at home. Make your own list. You'll be surprised at how skilled you really are!

If A equals success,
then the formula is
A = X + Y + Z,
where X is work, Y is play,
and Z is keeping
your mouth shut.

—Albert Einstein

The single biggest challenge we face as home workers, whether we own our own business or work for someone else, is balance. How can we balance the demands of work and play, of family and friends, of time and money?

Success calls for both work and play. If you work all the time, you'll go stale (as in the 17th-century proverb, "All work and no play makes Jack a dull boy."). All play and no work becomes equally stale—How can you relax from doing nothing? The tension between the two makes for a fulfilling life.

Why Z? That's a good question! We're open to answers.

First things first.

—Slogan of Alcoholics Anonymous

We have a lot of balances to maintain in our work and home lives. What do we do first? What activity needs our undivided attention? How can we do it all, keeping work and the rest of our lives in some kind of balance?

Some people are well organized and find it simple to set schedules and regimes. Some of us do not find this a natural way to approach our lives. Andy sometimes juggles his many activities in a reactive, haphazard way, and then wonders (1) why he gets so little done and (2) where on Earth all that time he had at the beginning of the week went.

This is frustrating! To combat it, establish a balance by making and following a to-do list. Then set priorities.

When we counsel business owners, we always try to help them establish their own balances, between production and marketing, between finance and sales, between education and action. These balances are tough for a multiemployee business—and downright difficult for the person in a home business who wears all the hats!

R-E-S-P-E-C-T . . .

—Aretha Franklin

Even though working at home has its distinct advantages over working somewhere else, interruptions can be a real problem. Like your dog barking while you're in the middle of a telephone interview. (Andi's dog, Ruby, has an uncanny ability for doing this.) Or your kids wanting to play computer games while you're rushing to meet an important deadline. Or the neighbor who thinks you've got all the time in the world to gab because you're just "working at home."

But there's a bright side to these and other issues facing the work-at-home crowd. Kids, relatives, and neighbors can learn to respect the fact that you're working, no matter when that is. That's why setting boundaries is on the must-do list of every home-based worker. Your signal of choice can be a closed door, a "do not disturb" sign, or letting your answering machine or service pick up calls. If you have kids or elderly relatives in the house, you have to be clear on what grounds they may interrupt you: a fire, a flood, blood, and so on.

What is worth doing
is worth the trouble
of asking somebody to do it.

—Ambrose Bierce

We all have too much to do—especially mundane household tasks. One way to deal with the sheer bulk of housework is to delegate as much as you can to other family members. Your spouse can do more cleaning, cooking, shopping. Children can perform tasks appropriate to their ages, even if very young. Ideally, you will do those things that you most like to do, plus your fair share of tasks that nobody likes.

If you don't take the trouble to ask your loved ones to help, chances are they won't volunteer!

There are plenty of tasks that are made much easier by a group effort. Think of a barn raising! On a more familiar level, if the entire family pitches in, raking the leaves or preparing the house for Thanksgiving or other holidays is a lot less wearing than trying to squeeze time out of your busy schedule to do everything.

What is success?
To laugh often and much;
To win the respect of intelligent people
and the affection of children;
To earn the appreciation of
honest critics and endure the
betrayal of false friends;
To appreciate beauty;
To find the best in others;
To leave the world a bit better,
whether by a healthy child,
a garden patch or
a redeemed social condition;
To know even one life has breathed
easier because you have lived;
This is to have succeeded.

—Ralph Waldo Emerson

This is part of the balancing act we face as home workers. On one hand we want to make money. On the other we want to enjoy our nonworking lives—indeed, this may be the reason we chose to be home workers.

Striking that balance will lead to a successful life in Emerson's sense. Both of us are writers, which automatically removes us from the ranks of the rich. We hope to succeed in these other, more important and more lasting areas.

If there are people
at once rich and content,
be assured they are content
because they know how to be so,
not because they are rich.

—Charles Wagner

There's no close link between being rich and being content. We've all known rich people who were miserable and poor people who were content.

Those people who are content didn't get to be that way by setting low goals or passively accepting things as they are. They set goals that make them stretch, they change (or try to change) situations that they feel need to be changed. They work hard, whether at their own businesses or as employees.

Three things
are needed for success:
a backbone,
a wishbone, and
a funny bone.

—*Anonymous*

You need a backbone to do what it takes. Self-employment or working without supervision takes a lot of self-discipline. Sometimes the work required to succeed seems excessive or irrational. But you still have to stick it out.

You need a wishbone to dream, to set goals, and to see where your efforts can lead you. Meaningful results don't come without effort.

Most of all you need a funny bone so you can laugh at the small disasters that always crop up at the worst times—the computer crash, the electric blackout, the delivery service that goes on strike. Then you can pick up and go forward.

Success is a journey,
not a destiny.
It should be enjoyed
through the entire trip,
not endured until
the final reward.

—Art Linkletter

At a business seminar review, Maureen Reardon, an artist Andy has worked with for several years, declared that she was successful because she *felt* she was successful.

That brought all of the so-called experts up pretty sharply, and led them to question the usual definitions of success in terms of money made and power acquired. Maureen went on to explain that she enjoyed the struggles inherent in being an emerging artist, and that the business skills she was slowly acquiring were an important part of her journey. Success is the growing process, not a final result.

Experience has taught me
that there is one chief reason
why some people succeed
and others fail.
The difference is not one
of knowing, but of doing.
The successful man is not so
superior in ability as in action.
So far as success can be reduced
to a formula, it consists of this:
doing what you know you should do.

—Roger Babson

Everyone wants to be successful in their work. Who wouldn't? The difference between successful people and the rest of the world is their willingness to do the things they know they should do, even if doing so is unpleasant, inconvenient, dangerous, or unfamiliar. They do it when they're tired, when others are relaxing and having fun.

You have to ask yourself a serious question: Are you willing to make this serious a commitment to the success of your work?

Roger Babson was the financier who called the 1929 market crash, making himself and his clients a fortune in the process. He was willing to go out on a limb and follow what he knew to be the right course even while all the other financiers were acting as if the stock market was going to rise forever. He knew better and he acted on his knowledge—his consolation for the mockery of his peers was his success.

Twenty years from now
you will be more disappointed
by the things you didn't do
than by the ones you did do.
So throw off the bowlines.
Sail away from the safe harbor.
Catch the trade winds in your sails.
Explore. Dream. Discover.

—Mark Twain

This is wonderful advice. Adventures are good for us. They can be small adventures, chances taken on learning new skills, or trying something unfamiliar. These small risks make life fun.

Most of Andy's sailing friends stick to the safe harbor, the proven and tried-and-true routines that they complain of. There are always reasons *not* to adventure. A business opportunity might be missed, or a client might be lost. The weather might turn. The engine might give out. Only two of Andy's sailing pals, Dean Plager and Gordon Chaplin, have had the courage and the wisdom to do what they wanted to do—Dean's Atlantic circle from Portsmouth to the Azores to the Caribbean, and Gordon's trans-Pacific sail en route to a circumnavigation.

Meanwhile, life speeds by. Will you look back on your life and wish that you'd spent more time in your office? Or will your regrets be for that trip to Europe that you didn't take, or the horse you didn't learn to ride, or the time you didn't spend with your children or friends? Depending on how demanding your work is at a given time, make sure you get similar doses of family, friends, and play time for balance.

CHAPTER 4

GETTING YOUR WORK DONE AT HOME

To love what you do
and feel that it matters—
how could anything
be more fun?

—Katharine Graham

How indeed?

This feeling has an important business role. If you love what you do and feel that it matters, keeping motivated is a snap.

We're amazed how easy it is to lose sight of this simple truth. People do the darnedest things—start inappropriate businesses, take jobs that make them uncomfortable on many levels—because they hope that eventually there'll be a big monetary payoff.

There won't be. If you don't like doing something and don't think it really matters, you won't do it well.

"Follow your bliss," said Joseph Campbell. Do what you love and the money will follow. If you are not having fun at what you do for a living, is it worth doing? Or would you be better off shifting to a more rewarding career?

A thing worth doing
is worth doing well.

—Lord Chesterfield

Perhaps. Listen to G.K. Chesterton: "If a thing is worth doing, it's worth doing badly." Or Frederick Oliver: "A thing worth doing is worth doing late." Or Barbara Ehrenreich: "It's not true that anything worth doing is worth doing well. The truth is, many things are worth doing only in the most slovenly, half-hearted fashion possible."

Some of these old truisms aren't all that true! There's a difference of opinion as to what is worth doing well, ill, or not at all. If it were clear what was worth doing well and what wasn't, managing our time would be a snap. We can all benefit when we start doing something by taking a pause and asking ourselves "Is this worth doing? Worth doing now? Or is it unnecessary?"

Work expands
to fill the time allotted.

—C. Northcote Parkinson

Parkinson's Law still holds. If a boss thinks that a task will take an employee an hour, then it will consume 60 minutes even though it could be done in 15. All of us can do more than we think we can—that's why working at home can be so productive. Nobody is telling us, "Take an hour to summarize that report" or "Get that information for me by noon." Without the allotted time, we tend to do our work more efficiently, at our own pace, with our own resources.

We can all do more than we think we can. Want something done? Ask a busy person.

Put your shoulder
to the wheel.

—*Aesop in* Fables,
"Hercules and the Wagoner"

Persistence, which we might define as hanging in there until it makes sense to stop, is a greatly underrated business skill.

Persistence isn't mindless grittiness in pursuit of the unobtainable. You have to have more than a feeling that it makes sense to keep plugging away. Persistence calls for directed activity, measured against benchmarks and plans.

Starting a new venture takes tenacity. So does working at home. You have to keep plugging along just the same way you would do going to an office downtown. Just because the sofa is there in the corner beckoning doesn't mean you can take a nap whenever you wish.

Business experts talk about the five-yard-line problem, where an entrepreneur quits when the goal is within his or her grasp. That's where persistence really pays off. Others quit. You don't.

If at first you don't succeed, you're about average.

—*Jerry Seinfeld*

Just don't take up skydiving.

With that exception, there's nothing at all wrong with trying and failing. We all do it—and sometimes it makes sense to try again. Sometimes it doesn't.

Think of learning to do anything difficult and new. We try and try again, because we want to be able to throw that perfect pot or make that tricky blind box joint, or even do something as simple as boil an egg properly. (That comes to mind because Andy has a granddaughter who is just learning about cooking. A lot of eggs have gone into that venture!)

If the anticipated result is worth the effort, then keep on trying. It's your decision.

If you think you can,
you can.
And if you think you can't,
you're right.

—Mary Kay Ash

Mary Kay Ash is famous for her ability to continuously motivate an independent, far-flung direct sales force, but her signature cosmetic line is nowhere near as impressive as her motivational skills. After all, what really is the difference between one brand of lipstick and another?

This quotation is right on the mark. If you think you can (sell, produce a report, run a home-based business, climb a mountain), then you can. And you will. That's the power of a positive attitude, a can-do mentality that bumps into obstacles and finds ways to overcome them. That kind of attitude produces accomplishment.

As they said in the old Air Force, it isn't the aptitude but the attitude that determines the altitude.

It is not enough
to be industrious;
so are the ants.
What are you
industrious about?

—Henry David Thoreau

Want to be productive, not merely industrious? Plan your work, and work your plan.

This will preclude busywork that accomplishes nothing. Some managers mistake long hours and frenetic activity for productive effort, and reward employees who spend more time trying to look busy than they spend getting anything worthwhile done. Andy was once disciplined for getting his modest morning's work done by 9:00 AM. His manager at that time, a certain bank vice president, who will remain nameless, wanted him to look busy. But Andy really didn't have anything to do, because the manager wouldn't give him more work. Talk about being an ant!

Actually, ants are pretty busy gathering and storing bits of food. Their industrious activity has a point: They want to survive, and ensuring a food supply is a critical task. No, they don't have a plan, but they act as if they did.

Nighttime is really
the best time to work.
All the ideas are there
to be yours while
everyone else is asleep.

—Jessamyn West

Nighttime may have suited Ms. West, but the most important question is, what suits you? The night owls in both of us flew away shortly after graduate school, but not so for our pal Roger C. Parker!

Author of *Web Page and Desktop Publishing Design for Dummies, Microsoft Office 97 for Windows for Dummies, Looking Good in Print,* and a score of other instructive and entertaining books on how to best use the computer, Roger always works at night. His preferred hours are 9:00 PM to 3:00 AM, a schedule he's found congenial for years.

Roger says that the advantages are obvious: It's quiet, there are no interruptions, his days are freed up for other activities, and he can call the other side of the world during their working hours. Plus, he can sleep very late if he wishes.

You can visit Roger's Web site at http://www.rcparker.com—any time, whether he's awake or not—to get design tips and learn more about his books.

Nothing makes a person more productive than the last minute.

—*Anonymous*

The last minute is very important when you have to manage your own time. When you work in a structured environment, such as an office or on a production line, your time is managed for you by someone else. When you are a home worker, you have to set your own deadlines and timelines.

One of our friends, management consultant Linda Fraser, breaks her tasks down into a series of small deadlines, and gives herself a small reward for reaching each one. While it may seem silly to spend up to half an hour every day laying out tomorrow's "last minutes," it works for her.

Linda has some impressive clients for her organizational development skills: the US Air Force's management and logistics center, a few major banks, a very large software company. They all are of the "hurry up and wait" variety, so she has had to learn how to juggle their demands. She hurries up and delivers, then waits for their checks—and for the next piece of the project. She tells us that if she didn't do this, she'd adjust her working pace to theirs—and probably would never have another job, because she'd never finish anything.

You can't cross a canyon in two small jumps.

—*Anonymous*

One of the annoying habits Andy has developed (and one he wants to warn you against!) is to try to do some projects in two or more small jumps when what is needed is one long burst of sustained effort. In his defense, this is sometimes due to family pressures—but more often it is the result of forgetting to take the time to set his priorities and consult the calendar. It takes a few minutes to get started, a few more to get up to speed—and there will always be a few interruptions—and time to wind down. Why do all of this two or three times?

Better take a giant leap and fly across that canyon in style. Allot enough time to do it right the first time because haste usually makes waste. As the great short story writer O. Henry said, "A burglar who respects his art always takes his time before taking anything else." If we take what we do seriously (as we should), we should take the time to do it well. Rushing into action without taking time to think about what we are doing is a great recipe for disaster.

Respect your art. Take the time to do it right.

Eighty percent
of your results
come from
20 percent
of your efforts.

—Vilfredo Pareto (paraphrased)

According to Pareto's Law, 80 percent of your results come from 20 percent of your efforts. This is a prime reason to analyze your work carefully and determine where your payoffs come from.

In sales, 80 percent of your profits come from 20 percent of your accounts. Which accounts should you concentrate on?

Focusing your efforts on the most profitable aspects of your business or job will lead to a much higher rate of success. Many of us, though, get so caught up in the daily hurly-burly of work that we never take the time to stop and ask ourselves if what we are doing really makes sense from Pareto's viewpoint. We just keep doing what we have been doing. This may make us feel busy and needed, but it won't lead to improved performance.

Life's like a movie.
Write your own ending.
Keep believing,
keep pretending.

—*Kermit the Frog,* The Muppet Movie

William James, a noted American thinker of the late 19th century, firmly believed that by adopting a posture of, say, enthusiasm, then the emotion of enthusiasm would soon follow. This belief underlies a large part of the positive attitude literature, from Dale Carnegie to the latest TV gurus like Anthony Robbins.

We think there is a lot of truth to this. We script our lives, working and personal, to a higher degree than we may at first admit. If we would be successful, we have to believe that we can be. Even if things aren't going well, we can still adopt the posture—dressing for success (so to speak) and trying to mingle with people who don't depress us.

We have a friend, Jack Falvey, who gives sales motivation talks to major corporations for $10,000 a day. When we asked how on Earth he could possibly get away with this, he grinned and said that every morning he looks into his mirror and says aloud: "Jack, you're worth $20,000 a day. You're worth $30,000 a day. You're worth $50,000 a day. At $10,000 a day, you're a bargain!"

CHAPTER 5

MAKING CONNECTIONS

It's not whom you know
but how you are known to them.

—*Theodore Levitt,* The Marketing Imagination

If you're a business owner, your relationships with clients/customers are *the* critical factors in their choosing you when they have a need for your product or service. If you're a telecommuter, your relationships with supervisors and fellow staffers are key to working together harmoniously.

How do you make sure those relationships are healthy ones? Keep channels of communication open. Ask regularly how things are going and if anything is needed. Initiate phone calls rather than just making callbacks. Make service suggestions—"Let me help by writing that press release"—rather than waiting for requests. Pass along useful information.

The time you spend nurturing relationships with clients/customers/fellow workers is an investment whose value will only increase over time—and pay big dividends to boot!

Something there is
that doesn't love a wall,
And wants it down.

—*Robert Frost, "Mending Wall"*
in North of Boston

For most of us home workers, solitude is both a boon and bane. It's a godsend when we're tackling an assignment that demands every ounce of our concentration, or when we're under the gun to meet a quickly approaching deadline. But sometimes, it just gets a little too quiet around home.

Home workers need to make concerted efforts to keep in touch with people—friends, coworkers, colleagues, and so on—and burrow out of their home offices on a regular basis. Of course there's always work to do and a million reasons to just keep plugging along with our noses to the grindstone. But too much time in solitary can be hazardous to your health—and to your career. Make a date for coffee or an afternoon ball game. Stay in touch with your pals, find out what's in the pipeline, and don't get trapped in your office.

The longest journey
begins with
but a single step.

—*Chinese proverb*

How do you begin the "socializing-for-the-benefit-of-work" process if you've just become a home worker? You start by putting certain activities on your must-do agenda. Attend a business-after-hours event sponsored by your local chamber of commerce. Volunteer for a local nonprofit organization. Go to trade shows. Get out and meet new people, either in your field or not, by joining a club, taking a course, or attending a house of worship.

If you're the shy type or if you just plain don't like to schmooze, take along a friend who has the gift of gab. Working with you as a team, his or her mission would be to break the ice and help you meet new people.

Because home workers are isolated by definition, socializing takes on an even greater importance. Once you've met someone, you're no longer just a name on a business card, in a newspaper article, or in the phone book. That personal connection will go miles for you.

Nice work if you can get it,
And you can get it if you try.

—Ira Gershwin

When you're newly in business for yourself, you might be surprised at how much time you spend marketing your product or service. But over time, these efforts pay off. You build a base of loyal customers/clients who keep coming back and a group of people who refer prospects your way.

This is true even if you're not self-employed. Your contacts can be of enormous help when you need assistance with a demanding project or if you're in the market for a new job.

One way to establish and expand your group of contacts is to network. You can do this informally (over lunch, coffee, or a telephone appointment) or more formally at events and trade shows. Make sure you've thought about what to say about yourself and your work so you're ready to gab with anyone you meet. Use your best manners, dress professionally, and limit your alcohol intake. Schmooze, but save your sales pitches for later.

The goal of networking isn't to see how many people you can meet in an hour. The idea is to compile a list of people you can count on.

Do unto others
as you would have them
do unto you.

—The Golden Rule

Keep this principle in the forefront of your mind in all your dealings with people. You'll never go wrong.

Remember your manners and always say thank you. People love to know that they've made a difference by doing something for you. Follow up all leads with a phone call or a note, making sure you acknowledge whoever gave you the contact. Shake hands when you greet someone and look people in the eye when you're talking with them. Always return phone calls and e-mail—one of our biggest pet peeves is the rude people who don't. Respond promptly to invitations and give plenty of notice if you must change your plans.

Treat people fairly and with respect, and chances are they'll do the same for you.

Strike while
the iron is hot.

—Geoffrey Chaucer

Timing isn't everything just in comedy—it's also critical to our success in the business world. Be sensitive to people and events happening around you. Know when to back off or change your plans, if that is most appropriate.

If someone has given you a lead, don't wait weeks to follow up on it. That makes you look unorganized and it makes the person who referred you look like a bad judge of character because he or she sang your praises when telling the contact you'd be calling soon. Always follow up on leads in a timely fashion.

Another must-do is to promptly say thank you. If someone has taken the time and gone to the expense to have lunch with you—not to mention that they've also given you their undivided attention for an hour or two and hopefully lots of useful information—take a few minutes to show your appreciation by handwriting a thank-you note ASAP.

God gives the nuts,
but does not crack them.

—German proverb

Once you've met people you consider prospective clients or folks with interest similar to yours that you'd like to get together with again, take the initiative and set up a meeting or an outing. Thanks to Martha Stewart, entertaining at home has become very chic; added benefits for business meetings at home are that there are no interruptions and they can be tax deductible. Just make sure that either your culinary skills are rated A+ or you know the best caterer in town. Hold on to all your receipts.

You could also start or join a group. We, along with several other writers, have our Scriveners' Luncheons every two or three months. We enjoy seeing one another in person (e-mail goes only so far in keeping us in touch), and sometimes we even talk about our work.

Book clubs are always fun, as was the Monday night sewing circle called Stitch 'n' Bitch that Andi's neighbor Alison Parodi-Bieling hosted. (In defense of her lack of sartorial skills, Andi suggested renaming the get-together "Stitch *or* Bitch.")

Ah, but a man's reach
should exceed his grasp,
Or what's a heaven for?

—Robert Browning

Andy's proud that he doesn't fit the male stereotype: When he's lost, he asks for directions. The same applies to savvy home workers: When we're stumped by something, we ask for help. Friends, coworkers, and librarians are all great resources for information—sometimes when we least expect it.

Trade groups and community-based business groups can be gold mines of information—if you know how to extract the riches from them. Groups on a smaller or less formal scale can also provide big payoffs. One we read about is the Digital Dames, a group of female executives in Silicon Valley. The Dames meet every six weeks or so, moving from house to house but never varying the format of their meetings. Everyone sits down and introduces themselves, saying what they need at the moment, whether it's advice, people on their board, employees, or money. Support is given, ideas are shared, e-mail addresses are exchanged, plans are made, and hopefully, deals are cut. Talk about reaching for the stars—and latching on to them!

By their fruits
ye shall know them.

—Matthew 7:20

Another way to build a network is to do some self-promotion. Write an article for your newspaper about your area of expertise. Teach a class. Join the board of trustees of an organization you're committed to. Volunteer somewhere—opportunities are everywhere, from public broadcasting stations, to hospitals, to community-service and nonprofit organizations. Start a program at your library. Get your name out there where more people will begin to recognize it.

Andy is an active trustee of the Women's Business Center in Portsmouth, where he's on call to help new entrepreneurs navigate the seas of small-business management. No only does he love working with owners of emerging businesses, he feels he's giving something back to his community. His enthusiasm is contagious—he's persuaded Andi, and lots of other people, to join the Center and get involved in its projects.

Don't ever slam a door.
You may want to go back.

—Don Herold

All of us have had experiences working with people who irritate us or whom we may dislike for whatever reason. Maybe they're Republicans and you're a Democrat; maybe they grew up in another culture or generation and have different values; or maybe they just communicate very differently than you do.

Whatever interpersonal obstacles you might face, always be professional and courteous to people. You never know when you may have to call them or work with them. Don't write someone off just because he or she is different—the problem could be your lack of experience or shortsightedness instead.

CHAPTER 6

ADMINISTRIVIA

The finest memory
is not so firm
as faded ink.

—*Lao-tzu*

Documenting activities may be a pain in the wrist, but it is very important that you keep good records of what you do. This is doubly true if you're a telecommuter with an off-site boss to keep happy. How can you prove productivity without records?

Get specific output requirements. What is expected of you? What are the norms against which you will be measured? What are the measurement criteria? Make sure to get these as clearly written as possible, preferably working together with your boss so you and he or she understand—and have a written record—of how your performance will be measured and can agree on these standards.

Part of this will be reporting schedules. When you will be measured is almost as important as what you will be measured on. The more often you are measured, the more your good work will be recognized.

Once these schedules are established, be punctilious in meeting them. The promotions you receive will validate your effort.

A verbal contract
isn't worth the paper
it's written on.

—*Samuel Goldwyn*

Sad but true—and sage advice for all freelancing home workers. At one time, legend has it, deals were made on a handshake. We're not sure just when this golden era occurred, but these days it's better to be safe than sued or out-of-pocket.

Get all deals put into writing and have your attorney look them over. Even verbal deals can have legal consequences (look at all the lawsuits in the tabloids!). A little prudence goes a long way toward avoiding problems.

Health insurance
and hospital gowns
bear a similarity:
You only think
you're covered.

—*Anonymous*

This is a darned good reason to read the fine print, a classic administrative chore. And it applies to all contracts, leases, bills, purchase agreements, and other documents that are used to negotiate or clarify terms. Some of these will be heavy legal documents. That's what you need a lawyer for—the mind-crushing details of most contracts are transparent to a well-trained lawyer, so you'll save yourself time and frustration by employing the right professional.

Your insurance broker understands the fine print of your insurance policy. Your accountant has a grasp of the almost incomprehensible tax thickets. Advertising agencies know what evils lurk within printing contracts, and so on.

Architect Ludwig Mies Van Der Rohe said that "God is in the details." Maybe he meant the devil is in the details!

Play it safe. Make sure that you understand the fine print.

There is no such thing as pretax profit.

—Arthur Snyder

If you're a home-based business owner, there's a line labeled "Pretax profits (loss)" on your income statement.

Art Snyder, a shrewd Yankee banker, used to tell his clients that pretax profit is an illusion. You can't spend it or invest it, he'd argue, because those darned taxes have to be paid before anything else.

He was right. You have a partner in your business, whether you want one or not. We call him Uncle Sam and he's not just any partner—he's the senior partner, the one with the most clout.

Much administrative detail is necessitated by taxes. If you are self-employed, you have to file quarterly and make deposits. If you have employees, you have to handle their withholding and FICA taxes (among others). There may also be state and local taxes. None of these are optional.

Taxes come first. Then you know what your profit is.

In this world
nothing is certain,
except death and taxes.

—Benjamin Franklin

Taxes are the price we pay for civilization, for roads, schools, and fire departments. Nobody likes to pay taxes, but only a political zealot would deny the need for them.

That said, there's absolutely no reason to pay more than our fair share of taxes. Tax codes are so complicated and Byzantine that nobody understands them, not even the IRS. That's why we need our accountants—to help us wend our way through the tax thicket.

Gerry Weidema and Steve Robinson, our CPAs, charge us several hundred dollars a year to prepare and file our tax returns. They make sure that we file the proper forms, maintain the proper records, and keep up-to-date with quarterly payments and a hundred other details.

We no longer worry about taxes. Gerry and Steve save us more than they charge. And freedom from tax terror alone is worth their fee. Get it?

Income tax has made liars out of more Americans than golf.

—*Will Rogers*

We have a pal who boasts that he deducted college tuition payments as a charitable deduction. We have another friend who gleefully asserts that his restaurant makes a lot more than he reports to his accountant. Others pad business expenses, slide personal expenditures into business accounts (one buried the cost of a new overcoat in the software account!), and otherwise try to hide income and lower their taxes.

This makes us cross, which doesn't mean we aren't tempted ourselves. We don't know if these people really did these things—but if they did, they aren't alone.

Too bad. A small business is a great tax shelter. There's no need to lie to minimize your taxes. Our CPAs treat our little businesses with great care, making sure that we deduct everything that is legal and nothing that is not. Make sure yours does the same.

Happiness is
positive cash flow.

—Fred Adler

The number-one rule of managing money is to take in more than you pay out. The reason so much emphasis is placed on financial management in businesses of all sizes is that cash makes the entire system work. You must have cash to buy inventory, pay employees, and market your products and services. You can't do business for long without cash; sooner or later you won't be able to find new investors and your creditors won't bail you out.

For home-based business owners, good cash management begins with your bookkeeping system. Get an accountant to help you choose the right system for you and then set it up. The cost is trivial. It will be returned many times over in better management decisions, lower taxes, greater profits—and untroubled sleep!

Luck is what happens
when preparation
meets opportunity.

—Darrell Royal

We sometimes hear small business owners complain about the bad luck they have suffered, the ill fortune that keeps them from meeting their business goals.

One blames lack of capital: Has she formed a habit of thrift and careful cash management? Another blames unanticipated competition: Has he taken the time and cared enough about his business to keep a marketing plan current?

We make our own luck, good or bad. If we're prepared, we can grab an opportunity. If not, the opportunity slips by. Is this bad luck or bad preparation?

Work only half a day.
It makes no difference
which half—
the first 12 hours
or the last.

—Kemmons Wilson

Mr. Wilson is the billionaire founder of Holiday Inns, a major-league entrepreneur by any standards.

He knows (and we do, too, if we care to admit it) that business success is a result of working harder and smarter than the next person—consistently. Not just when we feel like it, but day in and day out, year in and year out.

Writers are notorious
for using any reason
to keep from working:
overresearching, retyping,
going to meetings,
waxing the floors—anything.

—Gloria Steinem

Some of us welcome interruptions. Andy bundles this under the general heading of "pencil sharpening," a practice that any of you who make a living putting words on paper will be thoroughly familiar with. He creates interruptions if he allows himself. Instead of grinding out 1,000 words a day (his aim) he walks Thud the Wonder Dog, applies a bit of varnish to his boat, sends e-mail to his friends, or plays on the Internet. (Do you have any idea how much time you can spend researching on the Web?)

Some pencil sharpening is necessary, true. Research is part of the necessary balance between preparation and production. Sometimes gardening or mowing the lawn gives rise to a really helpful insight. A meeting can provide new ideas, new prospects, even some business.

Writers aren't the only people caught in this procrastinating habit. What is your form of pencil sharpening?

Out of clutter,
find simplicity.

—Albert Einstein

This wisdom crops up in a number of guises. William of Occam, a 14th-century philosopher, suggested that the simplest of a number of competing scientific theories was most likely the correct one. (This became known as Occam's razor.) Einstein urged us to seek simplicity. Insurance agents have been trained in the acronym KISS: keep it simple, stupid!

Keep strategies simple. Complicated strategies are hard to communicate, harder yet to enforce. Napoleon used to spend the night before battles explaining his strategy to the dumbest general in his armies. When Marechal Ney, his brightest general, complained about this habit, Napoleon explained that if General X could understand the strategy, so could the simplest private—and he would win the battle.

Take care of which rut you use.
You'll be in it
for the next 20 miles.

—Road sign in Patagonia, Arizona

Think of those ruts as the habits and systems you develop in your working life. If you have a home-based business you have to choose the business form (proprietorship? partnership? some type of corporation?), the accounting system (computerized? double or single entry? pegboard?), ways to get the work done, and so on.

Habits make work life simpler—we call this "doing business as usual" and "creating policies," and it usually is OK. Otherwise, we'd have to rediscover how to do everything every time we did it.

So ruts aren't all bad. However, take care which ruts you choose. You'll be in them for a while.

By the way, it is also important to know when you have to stop, get out a shovel, and clamber into new ruts! We call this "changing policies," "adopting new strategies," or "developing new systems."

CHAPTER 7

BEING YOUR BEST

I am a great believer in luck,
and I find the harder I work
the more I have of it.

—Thomas Jefferson

When it comes right down to it, the formula for achieving professional success is pretty simple: Know your goals, work hard, and don't depend on luck to get you where you need to go.

Hard work is most apt to pay off if it's focused and "begins with the end in mind," the second of best-selling author and management guru Stephen Covey's *Seven Habits of Highly Effective People* (Simon & Schuster, 1989). When you have a destination and time frame in mind, it's a lot easier to figure out how you'll get to where you want to go. With a course to follow, you'll have an easier time staying on track and be less likely to get sidetracked or lost en route to your destination.

Aside from the good fortune of being in the right place at the right time, there really aren't any shortcuts on the road to professional success.

Know thyself.

—Inscribed on the temple of Apollo at Delphi; attributed by Plato in Protagoras *to the Seven Wise Men*

How do you begin the journey to achieving professional success? Start with a look in the mirror. Not the literal one above the bathroom sink, mind you, but rather the figurative one within.

Get a pencil and paper so you can begin a SWOT (strengths, weaknesses, opportunities, and threats) analysis. It's a management tool used by business owners and managers to figure out strategy, and its principles can also be applied to individuals.

On your paper, make two headings: strengths/opportunities and weaknesses/threats. Take an inventory of your skills and your shortcomings (everyone has them), and your likes and dislikes, and put them in the appropriate place. Prioritize them and pick the top two or three from each column to work on.

Voilà! You now have several opportunities to pursue and goals to try to achieve.

You have brains in your head.
You have feet in your shoes.
You can steer yourself
any direction you choose.

—Dr. Seuss

One of the many keys to making your career a success or your business profitable is to take full advantage of your ability to choose what to do and where to go.

Because you have a brain, why not use it? Not just part of it, but the whole thing—the rational, planning left side and the more intuitive, emotional right side. All good plans (and every business and career needs one) have elements of both. You first need to set goals that fit in with your own values, skills, and emotions. Then you can figure out ways to achieve those goals using the resources you have available and can garner.

That's just the first part. Now you've chosen a course (as distinct from reacting to whatever comes along), you have to take action. We've seen a lot of great plans that were never implemented. Get those metaphorical feet moving! You can steer yourself in any direction you choose.

A jack of all trades
is master of none.

—*Anonymous*

Unless you are a handyman, who by definition can do just about anything that needs doing about the house, being a jack of all trades is a losing proposition.

True, you have to do everything if you're a home-based worker, from putting out the trash, to fixing computer glitches, to picking up your mail—but that doesn't mean you can't specialize in your work. In fact, specializing is one of the best ways to get your efforts favorably noticed by your boss or your customers.

Our friend John Blackford tried to promote his practice as a general management consultant with little success. When he repackaged himself as a "roving chief financial officer," he got a far better reception from his prospects. By differentiating himself from the jacks of all trades, he positioned himself as a master of one—and that sells.

Nothing is harder
on your laurels
than resting on them.

—*Anonymous*

In today's fast-paced work world, where job security is a thing of the past, not only do you have to do a good job—you have to do it better and faster than your competitors.

How do you stay ahead of the pack? There are lots of options to consider. You can improve your computer or marketing skills by taking courses offered by your local university, tech school, community college, or local adult ed program. Too long a commute or too little time for classes are no longer valid excuses for staying home from school, thanks to distance learning programs now offered by many universities throughout the country.

Make sure you're up-to-date with the latest developments in your field by reading trade journals, business publications, and the latest books. There's also a wealth of material available online. Attending conventions and seminars presented by trade organizations are other ways to keep abreast of what's happening in your field.

Be not afraid
of growing slowly;
be afraid only
of standing still.

—*Chinese proverb*

In addition to enhancing those skills you already have, make a concerted effort to expand your horizons. Nurture interests you may not have always had time to cultivate, and develop new ones, like learning a foreign language or taking art classes. Study a subject that intrigues you, regardless of whether it relates to your work. Your new-found knowledge will invigorate you, as well as provide a readily available topic of conversation when you need one.

Travel is another fun way to enrich your life experiences. So is taking up a new hobby or volunteering for scientific field research through an organization like Earthwatch Institute (800-776-0188, www.earthwatch.org). If you're one of those who's financially challenged, don't despair. With little or no pocket change, you can tap the resources of your local library, visit a museum on its "freebie" day, or take in a foreign film or two every week.

It is time to get drunk!
So that you may not be
the martyred slaves of Time,
get drunk; get drunk,
and never pause for rest.
With wine, with poetry,
or with virtue,
as you choose.

—Charles Beaudelaire,
"Enirvrez-vous" ("Get Drunk!")

Discovering something you love doing that's totally unrelated to your work can be an utter delight, especially if you're the hard-working, overachieving type of home-based worker. By making time for a favorite hobby, you can recharge your batteries, reduce your stress level, and maybe even add a few years to your life expectancy.

Andi began taking ceramics lessons at an art school when she was up to her eyeballs with work while completing her master's degree, and she still spends one day almost every week in a pottery studio—more than 20 years later. What's that got to do with her writing and editing business? Lots, because it gives the right side of her brain a workout and provides her with instant gratification from her work. It also allows her to take a short mental vacation from her other responsibilities.

Andy loves to sail, which he's only able to do a relatively short time of every year, thanks to our New England weather. But even if he's not out on the water, he's thinking about it, reading *Sailing* magazine, going to boat shows, working on his boat, or dreaming about what the new one will look like.

Out of sight,
out of mind.

—*Homer,* Odyssey

In addition to having a hobby, it's imperative to take regular breaks away from home and work. If your schedule only permits long weekends for now, then that will have to do. Just try to take more of these mini-vacations, and make a commitment to plan at least one week, preferably two weeks, away somewhere as soon as you can. Continue to do so at least once a year. The point here is to get out of your element as often as possible so that you can get some honest-to-goodness R&R.

It can also be wonderfully invigorating to go somewhere and not relax at all. At the drop of a hat, Andi would hop on a plane bound for Paris, a city she finds intoxicating. But she knows for a fact that two weeks in the City of Light would not be enough to quench her thirst. Maybe after a couple of months or so there, she tells her husband, she might finally be able to relax. At that time, she might in all sincerity ask, What home office?

Look to your health;
and if you have it,
praise God, and value it
next to a good conscience;
for health is the second blessing
that we mortals are capable of;
a blessing that money cannot buy.

—*Izaak Walton,* The Compleat Angler

Your mother was right about eating well and taking care of yourself. There's no better insurance for living an active, full, and long life.

One of the most important things we home workers can do is establish an exercise routine—and stick to it. Those of us who spend a lot of time in front of our computers are prone to getting "furniture disease" (when your chest slides into your drawers), our friend Trafton Crandall's term for the flabby and broad backsides we're liable to acquire from overexposure to our chairs.

We all know the benefits of moderation in everything, especially in reference to smoke, drink, food, and anything else that can harm us when we have too much of it. Or you could take Mick Jagger's approach: "It's all right letting yourself go, as long as you can get yourself back."

Training is everything.
The peach was once a bitter almond;
cauliflower is nothing but
cabbage with a college education.

—*Mark Twain*

All of us, at one time or another, need refreshment. Not just the kind we ingest or imbibe, but the intangible sort that stretches our capabilities, builds our spirits, and gives us confidence to do things we thought we never could.

No matter how old you are, it's never too late to learn something new. Sign up for a gourmet cooking class or start piano lessons. Take up a sport to build your endurance. Even though you may struggle at first, your skills and strength will grow over time.

Believe in yourself and invest in yourself. You'll reap big dividends over the long haul.

Improvisation is too good
to leave to chance.

—Paul Simon

Improvisation in music takes off from something established—a melodic line, rhythm, or theme. It isn't just a matter of playing random notes in a random pattern. It doesn't come easily. It doesn't happen by chance. Without understanding that base, improvisation is just discordance.

Paul Simon's music is improvisational. He builds on and takes inspiration from themes ranging from Afro-pop to Cajun to R&B, and far beyond. Is this due to chance? No! Knowledge and effort joined to talent lead to his wonderful music.

Innovation, creating something new from older elements, is a form of improvisation. In these rapidly changing times, we all have to be innovators, improvising new solutions to old and recurrent problems as well as new challenges.

Know your basics. Nothing else will lead to innovation.

Never invest your money
in anything that eats
or needs repairing.

—Billy Rose

Billy Rose knew what he was talking about—and his advice is still sage. Although he was a showman by trade, he made a fortune in telephone stocks in the early part of the 20th century.

Whether you're saving for the day when you can start your own business, travel to Europe for an extended vacation, or retire from work for good, you've got to make your money work as hard—or harder—than you do. Start by giving yourself a financial education, if you don't already have one. Take a course in personal financial management, read *Money* and *Kiplinger's Personal Finance* magazine, and watch programs like Louis Rukeyser's *Wall Street Week* on public television. When it comes time to decide how to put your money to work, talk with a bank trust officer or a fee-only financial planner. Like the plague, avoid getting advice from anyone who sells financial products on commission. They're hardly objective. If you're just beginning an investment portfolio, stick with mutual funds—their staffers work full-time doing the research necessary to buying and selling stocks, and making a profit doing so.

Better to wear out
than rust out.

—Bishop Richard Cumberland

It's no coincidence that "rust" is an anagram of "ruts," because the two words are closely related. Stay in your ruts and you'll be sure to rust. Stay active and involved—chances are you'll blossom and time will seem to fly by.

What kind of ruts are the easiest for home workers to fall into? Burrowing in at home is one. Working too hard is another. So is doing things the same way you've always done them, despite whatever advances in process or technology come along.

Follow Henry Ford's words of wisdom: "Anyone who stops is old, whether 20 or 80. Anyone who keeps learning stays young."

CHAPTER 8

BEING GOOD TO YOURSELF

It's true heaven
forbids some pleasures,
but a compromise
can usually be found.

—*Molière*

Be good to yourself. Andy says he's occasionally fallen into the Puritan trap of valuing work over pleasure out of some misguided notion of duty. About all that achieves is heightened grumpiness (due to a lack of pleasurable activities) and lowered performance (due to a nagging feeling that he should be having fun, too).

Compromise. Maybe you won't take today off—but you can take an hour for a walk or visit a friend.

Music has charms
to soothe a savage breast,
To soften rocks,
or bend a knotted oak.

—*William Congreve*

Most of us home-based workers have music playing in the background. Here in New Hampshire, our public radio stations play classical music or provide news most of the day, serve as a substitute for companionship, keep us informed on community events, and heighten our spirits.

Some days each of us listens to the oldies station, or country & western music, or even talk radio. Andy's children think he should invest in more CDs, but he's ambivalent. He loves the variety radio brings, the new music he sometimes hears, the odd or differing or rabid opinions that people have. Too many CDs would cut him off from all that.

We can't imagine working without music. What about you?

I can resist everything except temptation.

—*Oscar Wilde*

Small temptations and affordable luxuries make life fun. Give in to those temptations every now and then. Treat yourself.

You don't have to go to excess—be selective. If you gave in to every temptation, you'd not only get nothing done but eventually the pleasures would fade. So be judicious. Sleep in now and then. Your work will still be there, and you can finish it off later. Go for lunch with friends instead of working out, or vice versa.

Some people view shopping as a recreation, but feel that they shouldn't succumb to the temptation to go shopping. Why not? You don't have to blow the budget to have fun.

There is nothing—
absolutely nothing—
half so much worth doing as
simply messing about in boats . . .
In or out of 'em, doesn't matter.
Whether you get away or
whether you don't, whether you arrive
at your destination or whether you
reach somewhere else, or whether
you never get anywhere at all,
you're always busy, and you never do
anything in particular,
and when you're done there's
always something
else to do.

—*Kenneth Grahame*

If you have the kind of job that we have, where there are long, long projects that seem to take forever with no observable progress being made for weeks on end, then we heartily recommend adopting a wooden boat.

Why? Because there are an infinite number of small, short-term, highly satisfying projects that wooden boats require all year long, especially in the winter and spring. You can scrape, sand, paint, varnish, polish, rearrange, reorganize, make something that almost fits (and thus spawns a new set of finite projects), repair, stitch, caulk, launch, and retrieve. These are all satisfying things to do. Each has a clearly visible beginning, middle, and end.

Of course other hobbies afford the same satisfactions, because wooden boats aren't for everyone. You choose the one that best fits your pleasures. Just try to make sure that you too can have the fun of starting and finishing small projects. It will refresh you and make your work much more fun.

I make pictures and
someone comes in
and calls it art.

—Willem de Kooning

Andy makes pictures, too, but nobody would call his efforts art!

That doesn't matter in the least. Sketching is such a break from his normal routine that his almost total lack of skill is no bar to enjoyment.

Now, if he had some artistic talent it might be different. He'd take it seriously, work at it, try to develop it into another profession, and thus manage to banish all the fun from it. It would cease to be fun and become work.

His boys worry about his golf. He enjoys it. They can't understand why; if he were any good at it, they tell him, they'd understand his enjoying it. But as it is, they roll their eyes and sigh.

They miss the point. You don't have to be good at something to enjoy it. Especially if it isn't work.

Sour, sweet, bitter, pungent—
all must be tasted.

—*Chinese proverb*

Variety is the spice of life. Maybe we should say that the spices of life lead to variety—the careful mixture of different tastes and textures and techniques involved in cooking can lead to the most varied and delightful discoveries.

Both of us cook. Andi's desserts are legendary, her chicken salad inspirational, her soups the food of dreams. Andy used to bake bread until his children (who at the time were 8 to 12 years old) protested that they really, really, really wanted Wonder Bread. These days, he limits himself to being the breakfast chef (omelets are his specialty) and chowders, with an occasional pie to show just how foolish a grown man can be. And sometimes a loaf of bread. A few minutes spent vigorously kneading dough is notably therapeutic.

Cooking is one of the greatest recreations known to man or woman. Where is it written that meals have to be dull? Try cooking something new—you'll like it. And you'll return, refreshed, to your workaday life.

But though an old man,
I am but a young gardener.

—Thomas Jefferson

Gardening in all its varieties is a lifetime's recreation, suitable for any age and any level of physical or mental skill. We know a high-powered executive engineer who relaxes with bonsai. Andi pops outside during the nonsnow seasons and prunes, clips, digs, mulches, plants, coddles, and harvests various herbs and vegetables. Andy enjoys mowing his small city yard and finds that sitting on the edge of a raised garden bed plucking weeds is a fine way to think through a knotty problem. Both of us welcome the seed catalogs that brighten our dark winter days.

One of our clients, Elizabeth Brink, used gardening, including water and container gardens, as a respite from her work as a nurse. She now has turned her passion into an excellent home-based business, a growing profession (sorry about this!) called horticultural therapy. According to Elizabeth, she can bring the joys of gardening to shut-ins and invalids, to old or young. What a double blessing!

As an added benefit of gardening, there is always more to learn. A lot more. As Jefferson pointed out, after a lifetime of gardening, he was still a young gardener.

Dogs wag their tails
with their hearts.

—Martin Buxbaum

Pets are wonderful companions for home workers because they prevent us from turning into inert blobs at our desks. Both of us are dog lovers. Thud the Wonder Dog may be old, but he still is eager to please and even more eager to take Andy for walks. Ruby is boundless energy, a fitness dominatrix for Andi and her husband Mark.

If you don't have a canine coach and you work sitting at a desk all day, then make sure you get up and stretch at least once every 15 minutes. You'll feel better, less cramped, more alert. Lean back. Reach up. Wiggle your fingers. Do head rolls. Grimace and relax.

If you think
education is expensive,
try ignorance.

—Derek Bok

Many of our work-at-home friends have learned that adult education is a wonderful change of pace from their working routines. Our survey showed that they take a wide range of subjects: advanced computer programming (an artist!), French, Chinese history, creative writing, carpentry, small engine repair, photography, and teaching English as a foreign language. (A woman taking the latter course plans to travel to the Far East with her husband. She says she can find paid employment nearly everywhere they plan to go.)

They all cite the same benefits. Classes get them out of their ruts. Learning is fun. They acquire new skills and outlooks on life. They make new friends with older and younger people of very varied backgrounds.

Adult ed doesn't have to be career-oriented to be valuable. Try it!

The world is a book.
Those who do not travel
read only one page.

—St. Augustine

Wherever you go, business people perform similar tasks, though with a slight twist that makes it look on the surface as if they were doing something different. Business is business, whether in Rangoon or Rio, Rochester or Reno. This presents an opportunity to pick up new and better ways of doing your own job.

You might come up with a new business. Cappuccino may have been invented in Italy, but it was Seattle that gave rise to the fancy coffee business. Shrewd travelers noticed how prosperous Starbucks was in Washington and brought the idea back to Alabama, New York, Wisconsin, and beyond. Others noted the humble bagel in New York gaining wider acceptance. Bagel and coffee, anyone?

You can ask questions you wouldn't ask a competitor. You can find out how your counterpart 100 miles from home manages to market her business, sell his product, finance her expansion.

The moral is, don't limit yourself to one page when there's a whole wonderful book to discover.

Your mind
will give you back
exactly what you
put into it.

—*John Whitcomb*

This is almost true, but not quite. You will get more out of your mind than you put into it.

We can make connections between concepts, ideas, experiences, perceptions that aren't gained by putting connections into our minds. The more material we have, the more we have to work with—and the more new connections and insights we will be able to come up with.

Ever notice how fortune favors the prepared mind? We firmly believe that this is true. The prepared mind is well stocked with relevant material. People who work with computers in business situations are more likely to come up with new applications, new ideas for software, or totally new services like AOL than the rest of us, who have only a glancing familiarity with these matters.

A hundred years from now
it will not matter
what my bank account was,
the sort of house I lived in,
or the kind of car I drove . . .
but the world may be different
because I was important
in the life of a child.

—*Anonymous*

Priorities are: family and friends first, business second.

Material possessions and large incomes are fun but not of lasting value. They lead to wanting more and more.

Status doesn't satisfy for long. Relationships do—and that's where we urge you to put your greatest value. Surprisingly enough, or paradoxically enough, it will also free you up to be more successful in your career or business.